Family Conversations

Of Wisdom

Christopher John Gonsalves

"This story and book are dedicated to my Wife Jocelyn, Daughter Christine, Family, Relatives, and Friends."

Table of Contents

This story is about parents sharing their wisdom to help their children gain intelligent awarenesses and understandings needed to make important and successful decisions and choices with their behaviors and actions, with people, and with life situations.

This story is a gem and magnetic interest throughout for every reader.

This is a fictional story.

Characters include:

Adam – Husband and Father

Evelyn – Wife and Mother

Jennifer – Daughter

Paul – Son

Daniel – Adam's Nephew

Melissa – Adam's Niece-in-law

Ronald – Adam's Brother

Elizabeth – Adam's Sister-in-law

Parents of the Bride Melissa.

Introduction

I want and like to be responsible with my behaviors, actions, and decisions because it helps life to be more valuable, worthy, and important.

Adam communicates according to my awarenesses and understandings, all behaviors are learned whether negative and dysfunctional or positive and functional. I always do my best to learn from my mistakes and learn from other people's mistakes because I don't want to go in circles repeating the same mistakes. Ask yourself why a dog would go in circles chasing its own tail. This mistake doesn't include consequences unless the dog gets injured, but many human mistakes include consequences.

Some people perceive and consider humans to be animals, but I perceive and consider humans to be human only and not animals because of our mental abilities and behavioral abilities. Unfortunately, some people behave worse than animals because of the horrible and terrible things they do to other people (humans). People are capable of being more responsible, reasonable, rational, and reliable than animals. Humans are much more intelligent than animals. For example, consider our achievements with scientific and technological inventions, discoveries with medicine, chemistry, physics, and biology, and academic abilities and achievements.

3

Intelligent and important inventors, discoverers, surgeons, and doctors give people a better quality of life, longer life, and a satisfaction of existence, right, Evelyn.

Intellectual ingenuity improves our lives in many amazing ways. For example, serendipitous medical discoveries cure many health challenges or reduce painful suffering. I find inventors of science and technology, discoverers of medicine, chemistry, physics, and biology, surgeons, doctors, legislators, educating authors, and educating professors to be the most important and valuable humans humanity has to offer. They give the best improvements life has. Inventiveness, creativity, imagination, and originality are the treasures of human life.

Chapter 1

Today, Evelyn and Adam are planting trees in front of their house, which will continually sprout with life if they have enough water and sunlight. The trees will beautify the landscape. Afterwards, a conversation about different human behaviors began. According to my awarenesses and understandings, some people are responsible with their behaviors and actions because of smart, sensible, and necessary awarenesses and understandings. Some people are responsible with their behaviors and actions because of utilizing self-control. For some people, the reason of consequences is preventing them from choosing irresponsible behaviors and actions. My mottos are "being responsible with our behaviors and actions is a lifetime responsibility and being responsible with our responsibilities is a lifetime responsibility."

According to my awarenesses and understandings, rape and sexual abuse is about power and control. According to my opinions, rape and sexual abuse can also be about violence, anger, and/or revenge. Rape and sexual abuse are not about sex because sex is not about power, control, violence, anger, or revenge. Sex is not about hate, jealousy, or displaced blame. Sex is about human respect, sex is about human dignity, sex is about human pleasure and enjoyment, and sex is about human love. It is important to understand that our minds control our behaviors, sexual behaviors, and bodies. Our bodies do not control our minds, behaviors, and sexual behaviors. My beautiful love, Evelyn, I need your emotional love and sexual love to give my life a satisfying purpose and help my mental health. Evelyn, I always want to satisfy you with my emotional love and sexual love. Love is a mental need and desire. Sex is a mental need and desire.

It is important to understand children are not capable mentally, sexually, physically, or emotionally with consenting to any type of sexual behaviors. Children do not have and will never have the mental or sexual abilities and maturity to consent to any type of sexual behaviors. If a child is victimized with force, manipulation, or deception, should the child be victimized with discrimination, alienation, hate, displaced blame, or rejection for a lifetime? Some adults and children manipulate mentally vulnerable children to be curious about sexual behaviors they should not be curious about. Rape and sexual abuse should never be taught or learned. A person's silence is not consent to sexual behaviors or anything else.

No person's behind is rape-proof. It doesn't matter what the level of his fighting skills are, how old the person is, how ugly the person is, or the person's physical size. Nobody's behind is rape-proof is evident in the jails and prisons. People who rape and sexually abuse children and adults are raped in jail and some of them die while getting raped because they either get their rectum punctured or choke on their tongue, or get their rectum punctured and choke on their tongue at the same time. The nurses sew up their behinds with medical sutures for the inmates who live through the jail and prison rapings. People go to jail because of their behaviors and actions and not because of their race or skin color.

Adam, how are you feeling? Evelyn asked. Evelyn, I feel good because my mental health is intact. I feel good because I respect my dignity and other people's dignity. I feel good because I am secure with my sexual identity. I feel good because I respect different types of people and their differences. I feel good because I respect the environment because I never litter.

The reasons why some men do not have a woman, either temporarily or permanently, according to my awarenesses and understandings, Evelyn. Financial abilities, social abilities, personality abilities, and behavioral abilities. Judgment to identify availability and opportunity. Ability to create opportunity. Financial requirements, physical attraction requirements, and social requirements. Meeting and satisfying each other's needs and desires. Competition is another reason. Jealous interference and some people follow in a chain reaction with and according to other people's behaviors, descriptions, opinions, and issues. Jealous people follow in a chain reaction with other jealous people. Mutual acceptance is needed. People cannot control other people's feelings and choices. According to my awarenesses and understandings, people are attracted to the same gender because of voluntary choice and not because of force, manipulation, or deception. Some people want other people to be someone they are not.

Asking is very important to do. Asking for things is important. Asking questions is important. Some people perceive and interpret men who ask adult natural lady escorts for consensual sex to be rapists and this is not true. No behavioral facts to support this perception and interpretation. Adult escorts are about financial income for the ladies and sexual acceptance for the men.

Chapter 2

Adam continues, according to my awarenesses and understandings, violence is about power, control, anger, and revenge. Some people influence and manipulate themselves to become violent because of their expectations of other people and their expectations of different situations. Some people overreact and create unnecessary conflict with themselves and with other people because of their perceptions, interpretations, ways of thinking, and because of the awareness and understanding, they need but unfortunately they do not have. Violence should never be taught or learned.

Evelyn, according to my awarenesses and understandings, violent people and leaders only respect consequences and strength. Reasonable, rational, and smart people never need to be violent with other people for the purpose to communicate, never need to be violent to achieve solutions, never need to be violent to accept rejection, and never need to be violent to accept or tolerate situations that do not meet their expectations. Different types of rejection are included with some life situations. If we respect ourselves and respect other people, then violence is never a necessary option or functional solution with anything in life. Some people influence themselves to become violent because they do not challenge themselves with the endurance of patience and understanding of open-mindedness. I perceive and interpret violence to be an insecurity. Disagreements don't need to escalate into conflict and conflict should never escalate into violence. Some violent people end up in a graveyard or a lifetime prison cell.

According to my perceptions and interpretations, people having a dysfunctional mental condition should not have the legal right to be less responsible with their behaviors and actions than everyone else. For example, people committing crimes against children and adults who are evaluated as being mentally insane are not guilty according to legislation. Not guilty by reason of insanity is a dysfunctional law protecting dysfunctional and dangerous people from dealing with the necessary legal consequences. People have equal rights and people have equal responsibilities with their behaviors and actions. How is it possible for people evaluated with a mental illness and mental flaws to be given the legal rights to commit horrible crimes against children and adults? Criminals with a mental illness have more legal rights than the people they murder, rape, and physically assault with violence! As long as human life exists there always needs to be zero tolerance for criminal (unlawful) behaviors and actions in order to have and maintain (provide with necessities for life and existence) and preserve a safe and properly functioning civilization, environment, and society for humankind.

You know, Evelyn, it is very scary to know that we are at risk of losing our important and valuable lives at anytime, anywhere, literally anywhere. When a wacko randomly kills people, our responsible, intelligent, and pragmatic United States Of America government responds to prevent any more loss of important life. Do you know why people randomly prey on and kill law abiding people they do not know and who did nothing to give a reason to be killed? I can tell you the reasons, Evelyn. First of all, their mind does not work properly. They follow in a chain reaction with horrible destruction. They follow in a chain reaction like dogs off their leashes. Meaning they are mentally vulnerable and very stupid. I acknowledge that some dogs are smart. Do you know what mass shootings and terrorism are about, Evelyn? I can tell you, it is about violence, displaced blame, overreacting, and following in a chain reaction. Violence includes power and control to achieve a destructive solution. Violence is a learned behavior. Some people are self-absorbed with displaced blame because they manipulate and influence themselves to hold other people at fault for their abilities, choices, failures, life experiences, and other people's behaviors, whether appropriate or inappropriate.

Some people manipulate and influence themselves to overreact, or manipulate and influence themselves to be oversensitive instead of responding properly to their responsibilities, responding intelligently to different situations, and responding strategically to people's behaviors and people's different abilities. People manipulate and influence themselves to overreact with their behaviors, with their feelings, with their decisions, and with their policies. Overreacting creates unnecessary situations or escalates situations into negative dysfunctionality. Some people overreact and create unnecessary conflict with themselves and with other people because of their perceptions, ways of thinking, and because of the awarenesses and understandings they do not have. Assessing people and situations with rational and objective logic is much better than overreacting with inappropriate anger. It is much smarter and better not to be influenced with personal feelings or opinions and instead focus on considering and accepting the accurate facts. Some people are able to distinguish the accurate facts from inaccurate information and some people are not able to do this. Some people manipulate and influence themselves with their unnecessary sensitivities which may cause them to overreact. It is very important to understand the importance of not manipulating and influencing ourselves to overreact or to be oversensitive about things, communication, and situations that instead we can give ourselves more intelligent understandings to respond more intelligently, respond more strategically, respond more reasonably, and respond more rationally. We need to ask ourselves about what we achieve with foolish decisions and responses. I do my best not to magnify negativity and instead magnify positivity to the best of my abilities and to the best of the situation. Overreacting is an action and being oversensitive is a characteristic.

Evelyn, according to my understandings, chain reactions happen for the reasons that people emulate (copy) and follow other people in different ways. Some people follow in a chain reaction according to other people's behaviors and actions (whether positive and appropriate or negative and inappropriate) and follow in a chain reaction according to other people's descriptions and opinions (whether accurate and valid or inaccurate and invalid). A chain reaction (positive or negative) requires only one person to begin which sometimes becomes a trend. Some examples are the fact that responsible people follow in a chain reaction with other responsible people. Positive people follow in a chain reaction with other positive people. Dangerous, violent, dysfunctional, negative, jealous, hateful, and revengeful people follow in a chain reaction with and according to other dangerous, violent, dysfunctional, negative, jealous, hateful, and revengeful people. People self-absorbed with displaced blame follow in a chain reaction with and according to other people self-absorbed with displaced blame. I need to ask this question, if a person or people behave unnecessarily, inappropriately, or angrily with a person with no valid reason, should I follow in a chain reaction and behave unnecessarily, inappropriately, or angrily with the same person?

People are responsible with their behaviors and actions either because of their sensible and necessary awarenesses and understandings, because of their self-control, or because of consequences they will deal with or have lived through. Unless a person is being attacked with actual physical violence or responding to stop violence against another person, people do not have the human right or legal right to murder a person. People should only use enough response, restraint, and force to stop the person from continuing the violence. Does an innocent person deserve to lose their life or suffer because of a person's issues and selfish mind?

According to my life experiences, understandings, observations, and evaluations with different people, I have come to the evident fact and conclusion that crazy (disrespectful and dysfunctional with their behaviors, actions, thinking, and understandings) people are not capable of respecting other people in appropriate and reliable ways or loving other people in appropriate and reliable ways. Crazy people don't make any sense.

It is important for people to completely understand people steal in sneaky ways, manipulative ways, deceptive ways, and violent ways because they do not understand the importance and necessity of being responsible with their behaviors and actions and because some people think other people owe them something. Thieves who are not able to supervise themselves with responsible and respectful behaviors and actions, only respect the consequences of going to jail or prison and respect strength. Some thieves are self-absorbed with displaced blame for their abilities, their choices, their life experiences, and their failures. Intelligent people don't find it difficult to be honest (veracious) and morally upright. Learning and understanding the value of integrity will help people to be honest. Stealing (being a thief) should never be taught or learned.

Chapter 3

The family, Evelyn the wife and mother, Adam the husband and father, Jennifer the daughter, and Paul the son take turns reading the Bible each evening before eating dinner. This evening, their son Paul will read some information from the Bible. They are committed to this family tradition because the Bible teaches important moral values that are necessary to apply and include with their behaviors and lives. Religious and spiritual connections are good for their mind and their soul.

After our son Paul enthusiastically reads some important information from the Bible, Evelyn, and Adam begin communicating about the reasons some behaviors should not be taught or learned. Hate should not be taught or learned because people have the right to be different and have the right to their differences. Having the right to be different and having the right to our differences does not include having the right to behave misguidedly. Jealousy should not be taught or learned because people have the right to their different abilities, different achievements, different life experiences, and appropriate legal circumstances. This includes relationships, money, work, and education. Selfish jealousy should not be taught or learned. Selfish behaviors should not be taught or learned. For example, some men have a woman and do not want other men to have a woman because selfish jealousy has no boundaries. Some people who are not capable of achieving healthy relationships with themselves or healthy relationships with the opposite gender, do not want other people to achieve healthy relationships with the opposite gender.

Achieving relationships versus achieving responsible, respectful, and healthy relationships are very different. Being self-absorbed with jealousy comes from being mentally insecure and mentally selfish. It is important for people to understand the difference between jealousy and appropriate anger and the difference between appropriate anger and inappropriate anger. Displaced blame should not be taught or learned. It is important for people to understand that generalizing according to race, gender, religion, or any other reason comes from ignorance and lacking the necessary and appropriate awarenesses and understandings. People are not responsible for other people's abilities, failures, choices, decisions, life experiences, and other people's behaviors. Revenge should not be taught or learned. It is important for people to understand the difference between appropriate and legal consequences or legal punishment versus inappropriate or unlawful behaviors or unlawful actions. Power should not be taught or learned. According to my understandings, power should be replaced with different and appropriate abilities, different and appropriate authorities, different and appropriate influences, and different and appropriate strengths. Rape, sexual abuse, violence, and bullying are about power and control. Abusive control should not be taught or learned. It is important for people to understand the difference between appropriate supervision, appropriate guidance, and appropriate direction with themselves and with other people versus abusive control. Inappropriate anger should not be taught or learned. Inappropriate anger escalates into unnecessary situations, unnecessary conflict, and or unnecessary violence. There is a difference between appropriate anger and inappropriate anger. There is a difference between appropriate anger and jealous behaviors. All these negative and dysfunctional behaviors come from being ignorant, insecure, and selfish.

Jennifer and Paul listen with attentive interest. Now, I will share how I think about respect. Some people do understand what respect is and what respect is about and some people do not have the intellectual capacity to understand. According to my understandings, respect is about being responsible with our behaviors and actions. Respect is about avoiding to cause harm to people and not deliberately interfering with people. Respect is regard for the safety and well-being of people. Respect is regard for the rights, wishes, traditions, and feelings of other people. With the ability to respect ourselves and respect other people, then there is no difficulty in recognizing and obeying requirements and laws. When people are able to respect themselves, they will have no difficulty respecting other people. Some people perceive respect in inaccurate ways or perceive respect in perverted ways. Jennifer asks, Dad how come some people are not respectful? Smart question Jennifer, because some people do not 100 percent completely understand what respect is and what respect is about. Different people perceive and interpret respect in different ways. For example, what respect is for some people may not be respect for other people. Negative behaviors and dysfunctional behaviors come from not having the needed, necessary, and common sense awareness and understanding. People perceive and interpret respect, positivity, and humbleness in different ways.

Chapter 4

It is important to communicate some people are able to respect the help and accept the help that is given to them and some people try to destroy people, governments, and countries that are helping them.

Paul and Jennifer, it is very important to build and keep our character with continuous positivity, self-discipline, and structure because this will help us find ourselves as better humans who thoroughly know ourselves for who we are as individual human persons. Finding ourselves to discover and know who we are as a person is very important. It's no fun going through life being mentally lost. Life can be obfuscating and mystifying at times and through time I put the human life puzzle together successfully.

To move forward with improvement, people need to try different things that may work successfully or may not or may fail at first but succeed through time. The process of phasing different things into use requires the ability and willingness to accept change, adapt to change, and take smart and appropriate risks.

Some people live in the past with negativity and dysfunctionality (fixation with negativity and dysfunctionality) and go in circles repeating negativity, dysfunctionality, and mistakes instead of giving themselves the abilities to accept positive and functional changes and apply positive and functional changes with themselves. Within my abilities, I do my best to accept and apply positive and functional changes and adjustments with myself. I accept positive and appropriate changes and improvements for myself and for other people.

Not agreeing with, not liking, and not accepting with our morals, standards, and beliefs is not discrimination. A very significant difference between not liking, and hating. Disrespecting behaviors and actions can be discrimination. Having different abilities and different achievements is not discrimination. People have the right to their different abilities and different legal achievements. I evaluate people individually according to their behaviors and actions and not according to their race or skin color. I believe in myself, I believe in human people, and I believe in evidence.

As individuals and people of a country, we have the human need, necessity, responsibility, and common-sense human right to our boundaries, standards, and requirements with human behaviors, human freedoms, and human rights. As long as human life exists, people as individuals, governments, and countries need to always place boundaries (limits) with their behaviors, freedoms, and rights in order to be responsible and functional individuals, governments, and countries. People should never place boundaries (limits) with their legal and appropriate achievements. People need to be responsible with their behaviors, responsible with their responsibilities, responsible with their freedoms, and responsible with their rights if they want to keep their rights and not lose their rights. I need to ask, does our country or any other country on this planet Earth have the capacity to employ the world, educate the world, feed the world, house the world, and give free government financial assistance to the world? I ask is the United States Of America or any other country responsible for other people's abilities, failures, decisions, choices, or life experiences? Are we functional as individuals, as a government, and as a country if our behaviors, freedoms, and rights do not include boundaries (limits)?

Jealousy has no boundaries. Hate has no boundaries. Displaced blame has no boundaries. Generalizing has no boundaries. Selfish behaviors have no boundaries. Insanity has no boundaries. Ignorance has no boundaries. People following in a chain reaction according to other people's behaviors and opinions has no boundaries. Our legal and appropriate achievements should never be limited with boundaries.

Chapter 5

The next day, during dinner and after Jennifer reads some information from the Bible aloud, her father Adam began communicating the reasons it is important to respect the police. All people need the police to provide safety, protection, help with many different issues and situations, and maintain law and order. Generalizing the police because of the irresponsible 1 percent to 2 percent is the same as generalizing people according to their race, ethnicity, or place of birth. When the police arrest criminals, they are preventing the criminals from repeating the crimes, if the police get the proper support from juries and judges. Juries and judges have the legal responsibility and moral responsibility (concerned with the principles of right and wrong behavior) to apply appropriate, necessary, and prudent decisions regarding consequences and punishment with criminal cases of factual evidence provided beyond a reasonable doubt.

It is very important to respect the police and all law enforcement employees and cooperate with the police and all law enforcement employees at all times because when we respect the police we are respecting ourselves. When we cooperate with the police, we are cooperating with ourselves. I believe in intelligent common sense respect and I believe in intelligent common sense cooperation. Please be aware that not listening to the police directives and instructions can cause a person to exchange their freedom for jail time. Police responsibilities include many dangers and risks, and many law enforcement employees lose their lives because of being dedicated to providing safety to the communities they work in. The police and law enforcement employees have procedures and a process that they are required to respect, cooperate with, and apply with their daily duties. If we want the police and all law enforcement employees to help us, we need to understand the importance of helping them to the best of our abilities, the best of our respect, and the best of our cooperation. We need to ask ourselves, does it make any sense to try to destroy people who are doing their best to help us and help other people? Some of the many law enforcement responsibilities include identifying clues, describing people, describing things, and describing situations.

When I was at the library I found pamphlets containing information about rape, and sexual abuse, and about violence from the New York City Police Department indicating that rape and sexual abuse are about power and control, and violence is about power and control. This is an example of the police sharing important information to help educate people regarding different human behaviors. Paul and Jennifer, you know that according to my opinions, rape and sexual abuse can also be about violence, anger, and revenge. According to my opinions, violence can also be about anger and revenge.

If we are not responsible with our behaviors, if we are not responsible with our responsibilities, if we are not responsible with our rights, and if we are not responsible with our freedoms, we will lose our rights and freedoms. I am a winner for the reasons I am responsible with my behaviors and actions, responsible with my responsibilities, responsible with my rights, and responsible with my freedoms. I am a winner because I respond to people and situations with objective morality rather than the influence of personal feelings. Life includes being mentally strong in intelligent ways and being mentally strong in strategic ways.

According to my awarenesses and understandings, professionalism is about being responsible with our behaviors and actions, and being responsible with our responsibilities. I respect my responsibilities and I care about my responsibilities. It is about respecting ourselves and people. Professionalism is not about our feelings and the persons we like or do not like. Professionalism is about respecting people continuously. Supporting each other, helping each other and working as a team together will help to reduce the responsibilities and challenges we need to respond to. It is not smart to add issues and challenges to our lives. According to my perceptions and interpretations, life is not a game. Life includes many responsibilities and challenges we should be smart with and strategic with.

Paul and Jennifer, you know that according to my awarenesses and understandings, the methods and purpose of discipline versus punishment are different. Discipline teaches and guides people to develop and maintain self-control. Discipline helps people to manage their behaviors in responsible ways because of learning appropriate and positive behaviors. Discipline helps people achieve self-worth and make intelligent common-sense decisions. Discipline sets boundaries with what is permitted. Punishment focuses on deterring and preventing unlawful and criminal behaviors and actions.

Punishment gives people the opportunity to rehabilitate themselves. People can learn from dealing with the consequences of punishment depending upon the type of punishment, the severity of the punishment, and if the person has the abilities to learn from their mistakes, and the abilities to prevent themselves from repeating their mistakes. Some people go through life rationalizing their evil doings instead of doing their best to grow out of their evil ways.

Some people pledge allegiance to the gun and the knife instead of to the flag of their country. We greatly respect our country and respect our flag. We, as a family, put our right hand over our heart and say aloud, "I pledge allegiance to the flag of The United States Of America, and to the republic for which it stands, one nation under god, indivisible, with liberty and justice for all." We are always loyal, committed, and supportive of our country The United States Of America.

I am going to change gears and communicate about road rage. Evelyn, I know that most folks don't want to be locked up and caged like a wild animal. I sure and definitely do not. Road rage usually occurs with aggressive drivers and drivers with less respect for traffic laws. Some drivers need to communicate with their vehicle signals to prepare other drivers to brake, to reduce speed, to change lanes, and to respond safely. Drivers that do not utilize their vehicle signals properly and adequately to turn at an intersection, change lanes, exit from a roadway, or enter a roadway are creating unnecessary risks and unsafe situations for other drivers and for themselves. It is imperative for drivers to communicate adequately with their vehicle signals to give other drivers enough time to observe their driving intentions in order to prevent unnecessary accidents. When drivers activate their vehicle signals, I slow down because I respect their driving decisions, driving intentions, and human right to occupy the public road or public parking lot. I respect drivers using their vehicle signals. Speeding and following other vehicles too closely leads to many accidents. I do my best to keep a safe distance from pedestrians, bicyclists, motorcyclists, and all other vehicles. A polite beep of the horn prevents accidents and incidents with pedestrians, bicyclists, motorcyclists, and all other vehicles, but unfortunately, using the vehicle horn can be misinterpreted. Road rage can result in accidents, serious physical injury, or death. Sudden episodes of unwarranted anger can be dangerous and deadly. I ask myself, would it be smart or sensible to explode into a rage of anger despite a lack of apparent provocation or reason? It's a lot wiser to choose not to create conflict or choose not to escalate conflict but instead, reduce, minimize, and prevent conflict. I respect my life and I respect other people's important lives because life is very worthy and life is very valuable. I understand people have different driving abilities, different driving awarenesses, different driving understandings, different driving decisions, different driving behaviors, and different driving habits. Being responsible with our driving behaviors is a lifetime responsibility and being responsible with our driving responsibilities is a lifetime responsibility. Drivers are responsible to respectfully share the roads at all times. I don't take my safety for granted. To be a safe and responsible driver, I need to understand the language of all road signs and traffic signs.

Chapter 6

The next day, after returning home from working out at the fitness center, the family began having a conversation about drugs. Evelyn communicates drugs are for the purpose of curing or properly treating illness and disease. Let's ask ourselves about the things drugs do for recreational reasons? For some, it may create an opportunity for social acceptance. For some, it's a way to self-manipulate the mind to temporarily escape difficulties. For some, it's a way to avoid responsibilities. For some, it creates the opportunity to induce themselves into a condition of euphoria. Another reason is to feel mature. For some folks, it has evolved into an addictive habit. Sad to say but some folks think they don't have enough abilities to achieve anything important or useful. Please don't defeat yourself with your thinking (self-defeating thinking). Vitamins, minerals, and prescribed drugs are needed for our health. Consuming chemicals to play tricks on the brain with temporary stimulation is for people who choose not to challenge themselves in sensible and constructive ways. If marijuana is needed and intended to treat pain, how has it become accepted and available for recreational use? Some people know the accurate answer to this question. There are safer drugs to treat different types of pain. If people didn't have access to alcohol, marijuana, cocaine, heroin, and other junk, would there be less violence, less traffic deaths, and less theft? Some people become millionaires selling drugs while others go in and out of the clink, or forever live in peace with the spirituals. It is important to know how to harness (to bring under conditions for effective use) our freedom. Paul and Jennifer, you two may identify more reasons why people consume illegal drugs or destructive drugs. It is imperative not to take our safety, health, responsibilities, or freedoms for granted. It is possible for our actions to become habits and for our habits to become a part of our character.

Jennifer and Paul continue to listen to their mother. Some people communicate about other people's dysfunctionalities and flaws to help educate other people and some people communicate about other people's dysfunctionalities and flaws to help themselves feel more worthy and secure with themselves.

I was addicted to ice cream the way drug addicts are addicted to drugs. I am lucky that the painful meniscus of my knee told me I was eating unhealthy foods instead of my heart, lungs, liver, or kidneys telling me with severe pain. I learned my lesson when I could barely walk. So now, I stay away from ice cream and unhealthy foods to the best of my abilities. Jennifer and Paul ask if they can continue to have ice cream, and their mother Evelyn says yes as long as it's in moderation.

Later that day, their father Adam helps his wife Evelyn with household tasks, and afterward communicates that some people prevent themselves from achieving adequate, appropriate, practical, and intelligent self-confidence because of being self-absorbed with self-defeating thinking.

Some people describe and label children or adults inaccurately and the people being described and labeled inaccurately will accept (with their beliefs and understandings) the inaccurate descriptions and labels to be true and accurate. This inaccurate self-perception and self-interpretation will influence and affect how a person thinks of, and treats himself/herself, and how a person lives.

Adam communicates that having respectful friends, reliable friends, friends with good character, friends with good integrity, and friends with good judgement is important. However, there are some things more important than having friends. For example, number one is that we cannot control other people's feelings and choices. Example number two is that being responsible with our behaviors and actions is more important than having friends. Example number three is respecting people is more important than having friends. Example number four is being responsible with our responsibilities is more important than having friends. Example number five is achieving a healthy relationship with ourselves is more important than having friends. Example number six is achieving a respectful and healthy relationship with the opposite gender is much more important than having friends. Example number seven is not being self-absorbed with the issues of hate, jealousy, power, abusive control, revenge, inappropriate anger, and displaced blame, which is more important than having friends. Reliable respect is needed for friendships. When we are children and young adults, it is less challenging to establish friendships because we have more opportunity, mental flexibility, social energy, and time. My lifetime awarenesses, learnings, and understandings about positive and functional human behaviors and human thinking did not come from friends. It came from reading, listening to people through different media sources, self-learning with flexible thinking, and evaluating people's behaviors in person.

The reasons some people are antisocial, according to my perceptions and understandings. Reason one is social abilities, reason two is behavioral abilities, reason three is financial abilities, reason four is people cannot control other people's choices and feelings, reason five is a mutual interest and mutual connection is required, and reason six is because of their own choices and decisions.

The neighbor's dog began barking loudly because of another dog walking in the area. Jennifer asks why does the dog get easily angered? Her father Adam replies because the dog is not thinking properly. Adam communicates you know, it is unfortunate that some neighbors choose to bully their neighbors rather than focusing on their own lives. Some people bully other people because of their inaccurate perceptions or because of their issues. We don't need or want any of our neighbors spreading public hate or dislike about us or our children because of their personal issues. Public reputation being damaged can lead to horrible harm and danger for our children and for ourselves.

Chapter 7

A week later, Evelyn, our children, and I went to my nephew Daniel's wedding ceremony, and it is amazing and wonderful to listen to the ordained Pastor communicate the sermons and Daniel the Groom share his promises (vows) with his Bride Melissa. Daniel recites, "I take thee to be my wedded wife, to have and to hold from this day forward, for better for worse, for richer for poorer, in sickness and in health, to love, cherish, honor, and to keep, till death do us part." Then Melissa shares her promises (vows) with Daniel. They are promising a lifelong commitment of marriage. There are more than one hundred relatives and friends to witness and experience this special occasion. Adam's brother Ronald and his wife Elizabeth, and Melissa's parents are all there to give their parental support and guidance of advice.

After exchanging rings to signify their commitment to eternal love and a lifelong bond, the Pastor pronounces the Bride and Groom couple as Wife and Husband, and Melissa and Daniel share their loving kiss together. After the wedding ceremony the newlyweds, their families, their relatives, and their friends go to the wedding reception. After exchanging pleasantries, Adam communicates to his nephew Daniel and niece-in-law Melissa about marriage vows. A husband has the responsibility to love his wife, to responsibly provide for his wife, to protect his wife, and to lead his family properly. Real love requires that a man has an insightful respect for the equal dignity of his wife and to be grateful to her for her love. Always respect her, cherish your wife with listening to her, help your wife, make compromises for her, and give faithfulness and loyalty to your wife at all times forever. A wife is equal to her husband. A wife has the responsibility to respect her husband and compassionately help with nurturing the next generation. Women are equal with dignity, civility, and worth. Understanding, applying, and doing these things will help achieve a strong and fulfilling marriage with peace and security. Daniel and Melissa agree. When asked about where they plan to go for their honeymoon, Daniel and Melissa tell us, they will be going on a vacation tour through different European countries for the thrilling adventure and to learn about the different customs, arts, institutions, and achievements of the people in each country.

After the wedding reception, Adam communicates to his wife Evelyn, being unfaithful and unloyal comes from having a weak mind and self-manipulation. Instead, it is important to focus on being satisfied with the positives and pluses of the person you are together with. Focus on appreciating the person who accepts you and appreciates you for the person you are. Sexual lasciviousness comes from self-manipulation. The human sexual appetite comes from the mind 100 percent. The human sexual appetite should only include the one person you have a sexual relationship with or the person you are legally married to. All adults are responsible for their sexual behaviors, sexual choices, and sexual decisions unless forced against their will and choice. Evelyn, I made the right choice because I am with you. Evelyn, I am 100 percent faithful and loyal with you, and my continuous behaviors and my continuous actions are evidence of my 100 percent faithfulness and loyalty. Our decisions will determine our behaviors and actions. Love is a mental need and desire. Sex is a mental need and desire. Respectful sex contributes to and helps our mental health, emotional health, sexual health, and physical health. I am satisfied with you, Evelyn, for sharing your faithful and loyal love with me, sharing your important life with me, and always being my reliable wife. It is much more important to respectfully love one person with reliable faithfulness and loyalty than to be absorbed with human body lust for more than one person at the same time. Evelyn and Adam share their hugging affections and kissing affections with each other before going to sleep for the night.

Chapter 8

The next day, Adam and Evelyn are having another excellent conversation. Adam communicates it is important to value ourselves with proper dignity and pride. It is important to value our relationship responsibilities and commitments, it is important to value our home responsibilities, and it is important to value our work responsibilities.

It requires intellectual willingness to share our knowledge. It requires behavioral willingness to share our respect and kindness. It requires financial abilities and willingness to share our money and give material things.

Evelyn responds with agreement and advises her husband Adam that money cannot purchase intelligence, common sense, or reasonableness. Money can purchase better academic training with more challenging schools. Money can purchase healthier foods. Money can purchase access to more capable doctors. Money can purchase more reliable medicine in some places around this wonderful world. Money can purchase a safer area to live in. Evidently, money can purchase a much more comfortable life. For some people, money can purchase social acceptance. For some people, money can purchase respect. Does money help some people to achieve a reliable relationship with each other? Does money help some people to achieve sexual acceptance? Does money help some people to achieve sexual love? Does money help some people to be accepted into a relationship bond of marriage?

You know, Evelyn, according to my awarenesses, understandings, and perceptions, love is about mutual respect, mutual care, mutual faithfulness and loyalty with each other, mutual commitment and dedication, mutual communication, mutual acceptance, mutual appreciation, sharing time together, enough understandings to love each other in appropriate ways, mutual trust and love is about being satisfied and content with how a person respects you, cares for you, and loves you. Continuous respect and reliability equals mutual trust. Different people have different understandings about what respect is and what respect is about. Fidelity is your spouse not having sex with others which is an example of respect. An example of care is a person that wants to help you become and be your best. Love comes from the ways we treat each other, our intentions with each other, and our internal interest for each other. Love is a deep feeling of togetherness, closeness, acceptance of a person, and affection. Allegiance is loyalty and commitment to a person. With my opinion, loyalty is needed for trust to exist, and trust is needed for true love to exist. Being truly committed to you, Evelyn, I am giving my life valuable meaning and valuable reason.

Our expectations and requirements of other people can help us or hinder us. Evelyn, my beautiful wife, I am completely satisfied with the love you give me because my mind is satisfied. I have a satisfied mind because I educate myself to have and keep a satisfied mind. Some types of human connectivity are extraordinary. With my continuous behaviors and actions, I respect my own life, I respect your life, Evelyn, and I respect and appreciate the love you share with me. Respecting each other with dedicated and loyal love is important. I appreciate the value and importance of love. Understanding our partner's worth, qualities, and positives is important.

Evelyn, you know how to treat me with your affections. You respect and accept me for the person I am. You understand the importance of listening to me. I like your perceptions and understandings about life because they are smart and sensible. You are a sharing person with your mind and actions. I can rely on you for continuous secure love. Your love is trusting because of how you respect me continuously. You help people according to their needs. You are a winner with the ways you share your life with people. Your altruistic and empathetic love includes care and kindness and is special to me.

Evelyn communicates her appreciation for her husband Adam, recognizing and appreciating her positive characteristics and extraordinary qualities. You know Adam, some people feel and think a person has to live up to their expectations without having understanding and empathy for the other person's different abilities, different understandings, different interests, different goals, and different choices. When we search for our identity and find it, we can be secure or more secure with ourselves.

Chapter 9

Another day of important human life includes important responsibilities and important achievements. Life gets better and is better when we distinguish between inaccurate facts and accurate facts. Clearly identify the accurate facts and thoroughly understand the accurate facts. Having access to accurate facts of information helps people improve their awarenesses and understandings, which improves our abilities to make more intelligent decisions with our behaviors, responsibilities, goals, and everything else included with human life. Honoring the true accurate facts is very important.

According to my observations and life experiences, some people dwell on and have a fixation with their negative experiences, and dwell on and have a fixation with other people's negative and undesirable experiences. Instead of focusing on positive possibilities, positive probabilities, and positive improvements for themselves and for other people. I encourage people to give themselves the strength and courage to utilize the discipline of the mind for positive thinking.

Negative memories cannot find me for the following reasons. I am a positive thinker and choose to hold on to the positive experiences only unless needing to remind myself to prevent myself from repeating mistakes.

Patience is rewarded with positive decisions and positive choices. Life is not about obsessively concentrating attention on negative situations. Life is not about being self-absorbed with dysfunctional thinking. Instead I listen carefully to others. We are in control of how we think. We are in control of how we understand different things, different situations, and different people. Negative memories prevent me from being at peace with myself and at peace with people. Life is about achieving healthy relationships with ourselves, with our families, with our friends, and with people. I do my best to listen to my positive thinking. I do my best to listen to my common-sense understandings. 99.9 percent of the time listening is very important and needed to live life functionally, properly, and appropriately. Positive thinking can help activate creative thinking and intellectual abilities for building wisdom.

Later during the day, Adam decides to communicate about jealousy. Jealousy is not congenial to me. Some individuals have an addictive habit of being self-absorbed with jealousy. Jealousy is a learned way of thinking and a learned behavior. Folks have the right to their different abilities, different achievements, different life experiences, and different legal and appropriate circumstances. For example, this includes opposite gender relationships, financial success, work achievements, and educational achievements, whether academic or behavioral. I need to ask, is there a connection with jealousy and ignorance? Is there a connection with jealousy and insecurity? Is there a connection with jealousy and being mentally selfish? Some folks recognize selfishness with money and material things.

What about being selfish with thinking and being selfish with behaviors? With smart awarenesses and smart understandings, the mind can be free. Is jealousy needed or required to be competitive?

Chapter 10

Evelyn and Adam are out and about walking, listening to the birds' melodious singing, and breathing the natural scents of the flowers, plants, and trees. Evelyn and Adam talk briefly regarding different topics. You know true intelligence is observing things with logic. If we have an adverse emotional reaction to things said to us, then we need to ask ourselves if we have control over our lives? If a person thinks arguing is normal, the person must perceive conflict as being normal, and this dysfunctional thinking comes from ignorance and insecurity. Some people create unnecessary situations or conflict that only exists in their minds and not in reality. Some people use manipulation or deception to disguise their true intentions. Some people use strong behaviors, aggressive behaviors, and violent behaviors to convince and intimidate people to accept their lies as the truth. Some people perceive being respectful and cooperative with rules, laws, procedures, policies, regulations, and instructions as self-defeat instead of understanding the necessity and importance. Some people are not capable of respecting respectful people and respectful behaviors and actions. Some people restrict themselves from social opportunities because of guiding themselves with social and cultural standards or religious beliefs. Some people only care about their self-gratification instead of focusing more on giving their partner or spouse pleasure and satisfying their needs, interests, and desires.

Regarding education and occupation, I need to ask, is it wise, sensible, or fair to reduce test requirements for certain people if all people have the same responsibilities with a specific type of employment, profession, and career? Evelyn responds, no, it is not wise, sensible, or fair. Adam, I choose to study information, test the possibilities, and gain skills with practice. Qualifying for any position of responsibility needs to always be properly earned for the purpose of being fair according to each person's abilities, skills, achievements, and behaviors.

This evening Adam communicates with the family about what he understands. I have grown with my mind to understand narcissism and self-centeredness should not be taught or learned. Narcissism is more severe than self-centeredness. According to my perceptions and opinions, adults with these issues need praise, validation, and admiration from other people to feel they are worthy instead of building and keeping their self-worth and value as a person from how they think of themselves and how they treat themselves with their thinking. I praise myself in moderation. I validate myself in moderation. I admire myself in moderation. I value my achievements with moderation.

Chapter 11

The next day at home, in their bedroom, Adam communicates to his wife Evelyn, I am going to intrigue you with astonishment with these two poems I penned. The name of the first poem is "I Ask You Beautiful Lady."

I ask if I can communicate with you?

I ask if I can call you to listen to your beautiful voice?

I ask if you will include me in your plans?

I ask if we can date?

I ask if you permit me to affectionately hold your beautiful body?

I ask if you may allow me to respectfully kiss your beautiful lips?

I ask if you desire me to massage you gently with my tongue?

I ask if you need me to warm and love your beautiful mind?

I ask to share my generous love with you?

I ask if you want me to share my life with you?

I ask if you would like us to grow into being heavenly soulmates together?

I ask if you would accept a diamond ring from me?

I ask if it is possible for us to build a pulchritudinous life together?

I ask you to ask yourself?

I ask you, is asking important?

I ask if it will be nice to accept each other?

I ask if you choose to share your response?

"You Are Divine"

Your spirit is heavenly and vivacious.

Your character includes integrity and honesty.

Your enthusiasm is marvelous and ebullient.

Your conversations are engaging and agreeable.

Your empathy is special and important.

Your trustworthiness is authentic and consistent.

Your romance is loyal and faithful.

Your affections are warm and gentle.

Your desires are imaginable and attractive.

Your identity is secure and known.

Your wisdom includes understanding and common sense.

Your respect is dedicated and continuous.

Your chemistry is wonderful and astonishing.

Your life is worthy and dignified.

Your appearance is beautiful and sightly.

Your kisses are stunning and make me see stars.

Your love is devoted and true.

Your personality is likeable and loveable.

Adam, you are imaginative and original. I think open communication is needed to achieve and keep respectful and understanding relations.

Evelyn, I do what is necessary and right of my own accord and I am 100 percent committed to my vows and oaths I shared with you. My life is about being always 100 percent faithful, loyal, dedicated, and committed to you, Evelyn, because you are my wife, because I respect you, and because I respect myself.

Chapter 12

The family listens to Evelyn read some great moral principles from the Bible. After Evelyn shares nutrition for the mind, the family begins feeding themselves with physical nutrition, which includes baked salmon, boiled broccoli, and baked sweet potatoes.

Adam begins the conversation. I guide myself with moral principles because I learned to understand the difference between right and wrong with my thinking, perceptions, interpretations, behaviors, and actions. For example, I am not entertained with inappropriate and unlawful behaviors and actions. I am not entertained seeing people being victimized with sexual violence, sexual abuse, physical violence, physical abuse, mental abuse, emotional abuse, or financial abuse in real life or in the media. Is it practical and logical for some people to be entertained with other people's dysfunctionality, weaknesses, vulnerabilities, and pain? Is it human, appropriate, or healthy for adults to be entertained with observing or knowing about people being raped, sexually abused, or victims of violence? Should people magnify other people's negative experiences into lifetime vulnerabilities? Human dignity and human reason are entertaining to me. Jennifer, Paul, and Evelyn respond with agreement.

Now I would like to communicate about positive entertainment. My favorite singers are Elvis Presley and Connie Francis for many excellent reasons. For the reason of what they sang about. For the reason of the ways they sing with their voice. For the reason, their feelings and communication matched with the content (lyrics) of each song. For the reason of the chosen musical instruments used and how the musical instruments were played. For the reason of the special, extraordinary, and different creativity and skillfulness of their singing and musical instruments. For the reason of the team spirit, team support, and chemistry connection the background singers shared with the lead singers. For the reason of the care included with their singing. Listening to their songs helps me relax and distracts me from my worries. True relaxation feels naturally wonderful. Relaxing can bring about clever ideas and deeper understandings to help build knowledge and wisdom.

If I want a hearty laugh, I don't need to go to the dentist for laughing gas (nitrous oxide) instead, I pay attention to "The Three Stooges." I like "The Three Stooges" because they dive right into the action. The creative scenarios create an abundance of humor that tickle my mental funny bone like no other. Nothing makes me laugh more. Their humor and originality are magnificent. I'm a happy-go-lucky nostalgist and enthusiast.

The same day and after Evelyn finished feeding the family dogs and family cats, Adam communicates, you know, Evelyn, I did not understand the importance of stretching exercises (proper stretching) for physical health and flexibility until I went to a physical therapist with excruciating back pain. Through time, I added more stretching exercises to my weekly routine. As you are aware, I do some daily stretching exercises which helps to get me through each day with flexibility and mobility. Proper stretching has prevented the need for back surgery, use of a cane, walker, or wheelchair. Getting enough sleep, doing muscle strengthening exercises, and proper stretching is like medicine for me.

Flossing is another thing I learned to understand the importance and necessity of after reading an article (located in a dentist office), about how much mouth health and gum health affect heart health. Flossing significantly helps with improving and maintaining mouth health, gum health, and good breath. As you know Evelyn, I brush my teeth first, then floss between all of my teeth, and finish with cleaning my tongue with a tongue scraper.

Stretching and flossing add comfort to my life. Taking care of our hygiene needs is essential. Different people have different hygiene needs and have different hygiene standards. Being conscious of ourselves is important as long as we are not excessively focused on our physical appearance.

Conclusion

The family understands there is a difference between the definition of things and what things are about. Adam communicates with the family, what things are about explore deeper into the meaning, and not just the basic definition. What things are about includes reasons, causes, purpose, and specific facts and details.

Evelyn listens and responds, that is right. Evelyn communicates to Adam and the children, life is not a game because life is more serious than a game and life is more important than a game. I acknowledge that situations of competition can be similar to a game of chess because they each require eliminating people (not with criminal and unlawful actions) in real life and eliminating chess players to conclude with the same goal of winning. According to my perspicaciousness, life is a strategic responsibility.

Parents respecting each other and listening to each other influences and teaches their children to learn to respect their parents and listen to their parents. Life is nice and life is nicer with positive behaviors. I am always doing my best to increase my awarenesses and understandings about myself, about you, Evelyn, and about other people. How our minds work, how we think, how we perceive and interpret communication, situations, and people will determine how we live and the continuous direction of our lives.

Some people are so lost with their mind that I describe them as a mental mess. Some people live through life having dysfunctional behaviors, habits, and manners. I am living through life being functional with my behaviors, habits, and manners.

I open my mind to evaluate human behaviors. According to my opinion the learning process includes accepting information and or behaviors, understanding information and or behaviors, and applying information and or behaviors with ourselves. Our reading, studying, observations of, involvement with, participation in, and experience with are all included with the process of learning. Many decisions need to be well thought out if we want to prevent being injudicious with our responses and actions. I like to learn to gain knowledge through information, studying, and practical experience which helps me to be sagacious with my decisions and judgment. I am continuously learning the awarenesses and understandings about human behaviors. Learning good and helpful things helps us to improve ourselves and improve our lives. We understand humans have different learning abilities and strengths, learn in different ways, learn with different methods, and learn at different paces. The children listen to their parents and agree.

Life is beautiful, life is special, and life is wonderful. Nothing is better than achieving a successful life with ourselves, with our spouse, with our family, with our friends, and with every person we interact with for personal reasons and business reasons. Succeeding with positivity and functionality makes us winners and able to experience the true treasures of life.

I like living my life in an unpretentious way because I am not phony with myself or with people. I like to be real and genuine with myself and with people. I like living my life in an unostentatious way because I have nothing to gain with being showy or obtrusive. Grandiosity is not needed to be successful.

I choose to be at peace with myself because I want to always be at peace with you, Evelyn, be at peace with my family, be at peace with my relatives, be at peace with my friends, be at peace with my neighbors, be at peace with the people I work with, and be at peace with all human beings always. I love life because I'm at peace with myself and human life. Evelyn and I share our wisdom because we care for humans. It is our belief that our abilities, choices, decisions, awarenesses, and understandings guide the pathway of our amazing life. I like to stir my imagination to inspire creative thinking, evoke vivid ideas, and enliven a sense of wonder. Evelyn, your love is medicine for me. We pray in silence for peace and calm now. May the Lord bless all of us.

Questions or comments, please email

humanbehaviors100@gmail.com

www.ingramcontent.com/pod-product-compliance
Lightning Source LLC
Chambersburg PA
CBHW051335120626
46547CB00016B/2549